Suburbs of my Childhood

Bill Vartnaw

Beatitude PRESS
BERKELEY, CALIFORNIA

Book and Cover Designed by Douglas Rees
Photo on page 71 by Jim Scott, circa 1989

Printed in the United States of America
By Beatitude Press, Berkeley, California
All rights reserved.

ISBN: 978-0-9815047-0-4

Grateful acknowledgment is made to the following magazines in which these poems first appeared, sometimes in slightly different forms: *Paper Pudding, Lovelights, Minotaur, Haight Ashbery Literary Journal, Tunnel Road 2,   Berkeley Works 3, Plunk!, Awaate, Underground, Zam Bomba, North Coast (Literary) Review*, Listen and Be Heard's *Poem of the Day*, listenandbeheard.net and About.com Poetry (Spring Poems). I also want to thank the several magazines who accepted some of these poems, but then could not afford to publish the next issue. It still meant a lot. "The Goddess of Walnuts" appeared in Petaluma Poetry Walk 10-Year Anthology, 2007, PPW Press.

Contents:

To Bridget
This is the Preface
before We were born

THE PURSUIT

The part I that leads us in
to participation. The thing-in-itself,
of itself, is always & never
complete. A lover like Don Juan, forever
at the mercy of his next conquest,
prefers evolution to the power
of his own magic. "Marriage," she said,
as if it were entrapment. What I mean
is only the beginning. A form
we partake & make ours. A baby's hand,
those pudgy little digits of desire,
learning to clutch your index, yearns & grows
longer, gets dirty to get washed into
Grandma's knitted mittens, worn out
fielder's glove. Don Juan speaks highly of
refining his "method" when he's out
with the boys. Attractions never leave us.
Though we may muddy the water, our thirst
clearly turns into temptation. I come to
this life to leave my fingerprints.

The Grid

it is the grid
we lay over experience
to understand
i was 16
before they told me

i couldn't see clearly
what does that mean
i wanted to drive
there are laws
a policeman once told me

"it's a privilege to drive
on the streets
& highways of CA"
then he handed me
a 25-dollar ticket

"officer, i'm wearing
glasses
& i never saw
that no left turn sign
honest"

in my younger days,
i could feel a baseball
leave the bat
& follow it into my glove
afterwards,

i made a spectacle
of myself
it became mechan-
ical.
i lost confidence

not that there is anything
wrong with 20/20 vision
it's one more world
that takes getting used to
like me

When We Are

when we are
facing lions
our hearts toll
unexpectantly loud
waking the entire village
where each of us
lives

when we are
facing lions
all the ambitious
door to door salesmen
of thoughtful enterprise
are strong-armed
and run out of town
by the local inhabitants

when we are
facing lions
all the prisoners
are given amnesty,
guns, keys to the city
and commands of the front
lines

when we are
facing lions
all the women
retreat to the church
excommunicate the priest
barricade the door
and become the pure source
of divine inspiration

when we are
facing lions
all the men
complete a surge
of energy direct
that was completely lost
to their business shapes
as usual

LABORATORY CONDITIONS

When it began I wasn't even
four feet high. I cried hysterically.
No one understood the what-for,
the how-to was easy:

we'd charge the pillbox on the bunker.
Blameless in our passions, we'd weave
between the explosions we saw
echo real in our throats. "My hero!"

She reversed the process in just one week
of Easter. Quiet like a plastic surgeon,
she changed to the "after" picture
in the newspaper: her pink petal pushers

by a pool. There were bound to be complications…
Not to say the operation wasn't a success,
but I still have a hard time explaining
the importance of the fat lady I use to know

or that pretty girl with the remodelled face
& a mind of her own
left with it, taking a good part of my life
in that suitcase with her. She did leave me

these pink petal pushers. & look!
They fit my arms like a straight-jacket.

FOOTBALL HERO

She kicks high
within me

Within me, her cutesy dance
beckons a stadium of emotions
to focus

Enchantress with a megaphone:
"Come on, show your spirit!
Let the team hear you…"
I do not need to hear
She watches & we are one

What I do is important
The P.A. will call out my name
It will fill up the air
She will hear it & remember

She kicks high
shows her panties
embroidered: Win! or War!
I cannot tell, swelled

I want to yell: tie me to the goalpost
Look ahead & see the ambulance,
my knee enters his kidneys
She kicks high

We are one & they do not matter
til knee finds his flesh
a matter that shatters dreams
& I am alone
                    with victory.

THE UNMOVIE

not

                cop chases
tiresqueel around skyscrapered

blasting

                        intense focus/darkness

                                      bigger than

the reel

                            an investment not
                                    to see each

                frame/the spaces

the pull the eyes project

                                    shrillsirens

follow the getaway,

              life/death

                            through hindsight

via this smooth why

                          not

Variations on a Theme by Rimbaud & Olson

I

Sugar pine bark
made into boats

Three-pronged needles
fill the forest floor—
the kept trail is swept
by traffic...
                    O saison, O chateaux!

What soul is without desire?

Magic, the study
memory makes:
petals from apple trees
swirl on Gravenstein Road...

Morning stretches
its black midnight neck
to project
this cock's chant
the chill waking wind
pushing the pine's perfume...

Ah! just a whiff—
happiness, the charge
feeds body & soul...
All effort ceases
as living energies release...

I've walked through seasons
into a forest
to find a home
the hour of death
will not trespass...

II

Sugar pine bark boats
float with mast of twig...

Three pronged needles
keep clear
                        of "clean" trail
sweeping through forest floor...
                O saison, O chateaux!

What soul is without sun & moon?

Magic, a study
riddled with green—
photosynthesis?
a picture of white blossoms
blowing at noon, etc.,
past Sebastopol asphalt—
the road to Russian River redwoods...
My memory is at home near Petaluma

I salute the crowing cock
that wakes me, the shock of feathers
shimmering—
                        the light
never without shadows & yet
the moment free
from envy...
                O saison, O chateaux!

Ah happiness...
how complacent I can be—
my living energies, a continuous charge
alternating on a round, spinning magnet
These "seizing seasons" make such
a comfortable fence
for forest's continuous change...

even the hands of the hour of death pass by
as if in charmed flight...

III

Sugar pine bark boats float
down to Feather River...
Twig masts
the last of a relived childhood memory
disappear in a rush of white winter snow
                              clear into summer
—bedrocks glazed with spring...

The needles three-pronged scent,
it is clear:
this path has no beginning or end
but passes the spaces where tall trees grow...
                O saison, O chateaux!

What soul is without within?

Petaluma smelled of eucalyptus
& backyard roses A magic study:
poetry—a place I also call
home, free of the clock's bungling...

Cocks crow at dusk—
they show no shame,
their high-pitched call
                takes the shape of the valley
& disappears in the shadows silence makes...

Wind charges through shimmering
leaves, shaking boughs
crack... I note a change
I miss a million transitions...

There can be no separation
no moment's part in eternity...

& yet, there is

Still Life with a Cat

How spastic the cat's fancy.
No, that's not it. From another
perspective, there are so many ways
to look. It has been years since I

last saw his face watching a kitten
grow. No. He couldn't. Not really. I watched
for a day, days on end. Distracted by
purrs & fur & whiskers & canines &

claws & commercials on TV. There
is no time-lapse to get bigger in. No,
at least, not now. *How plastic the fast can
see.* Close. Not quite. The kitten got bigger,

became a cat. I concluded it
grew within me, without me. Between us,
we created a moment or shared
a source of one... Oh yes, I remember:

How elastic the past can be.
Now we talk; that time we
shared grew in her own
time. Awkward, we move closer—

a past we used, to know
(from another perspective...) &
further from this being that comes
between us... which we can't. As yet.

SUSPENDED ANIMATION

Saturday morning. Cartoontime.
Twenty years ago. How the young are exposed
to changes. Bugs. My dad & I laughing
together. How simple
it is to make him laugh. So much
like a child. So much like me.
I marvel, taken aback (perhaps the first time)
how unfamiliar you are. There are stock gimmicks
set up with repetition. We are led to expect
casual impossibility. That'd be funny…
(enough to get his goat.) Then WHAMMO!
I, too, caught in context like a stuttering pig, jiggling
the lock, the door of the belly, letting
go. Grampa would've never sat with him
as he with his child watch make-believe
bunny make asses out of a world with teeth
& guns. The old world is more serious,
self-centered like Yosemite Sam. You can hear
that chomping everywhere. A carrot's point dulls
into a characteristic question. "Now I gotchu
you louzee wabbit!" Though he never does,
not one of us does. Something will happen, is
happening now. You can be sure.
The unexpected. Different as I am from you &
you from your father. I am not progress
but something less pointed like Skylab returning
to Earth, something more akin to pulling
a rabbit into a poem & continuing
on to the next trick…

FLOWERS

its seed
as the sun
in its fullness
thrive
on its own
amidst an atmosphere
of others

it needs them
indiscriminately

it needs them

the water's moisture
the earth's soil
the sun's radiance

it truly needs them
and receives their gifts
graciously
but keeps itself
distant
(a space not measured
by mile or meter)
and became slave
to no lesser passion
than its own perfect gift
the bloom

WIND

wind
jostles
eucalyptus

wind & words

30-foot (plus)
structures
sway & shimmer
almost weightless
against blue

trees
at play
(or surviving?)

some poems
push past
the literal
& acknowledge it

unseen
roots hold
(sway)

sinews
of sap,
the ooze of
unconscious
knowing

a ring
(marks
the growing
season)
peals
when true

Every Work of Art Needs a Title

I
yea
like being greedy
and drilling for oil
and not knowing the earth
is some child's balloon
til POP!

TH TH TH TH TH TH TH TH TH TH TH

all around the universe
all the crying

II
why are bombs so popular?

III
on his deathbed
(his reservations were late
death came as an inconvenience)
her face was absent
but thoughts of her remained
scattered like dust

IV
Plink
(the moth hits the light bulb)
Plink
            Plink

V
he was one person
she was another person
living became a continual process
of integrating and segregating
this information
they chose to call it love

CONTACT SPORT

The choices we made to lose touch...

To become phantoms. Another person. I stood in a crowd
looking up. The lead ball swung by the crane. Boom!
There is a fascination. How much the structure can take.
How the impact turns to rubble below. Dust flies.
We are made of this. Up from the foundation, the framework
often bends to unlikely degrees before collapsing. Boom!
Each rivet registers each blow. One by one, the crowd leaves
stunned by the building's strength. The machine's power.
The waste. The marked absence in the making. In time,
the debris will be cleaned up & hauled away. To new purposes
or simply junked. The clean space will hardly seem natural.

> I think of Kneeland's quiet intensity. Driving
> down the middle. The foul.
> The anger. Drawing us closer
> into the bounds of group & self-consciousness
> Thompson's laughter
> after a set-shot: *swish!*
> It was psychic
> how some plays were so pretty,
> pick & roll:
> a pass the moment I broke to the basket.
> We sense each other's moves,
> keep moving: the magic! We grow,
> let each other know immediately.
> There is an agreement between us:
> as one gets better, we all improve
> or 'the game' loses...interest
> Everhart became a threat from the corner.
> Hearney banks the ball off the backboard.
> Ankles & elbows reach for the rebound:
> "Take it back!"

Our memory changes things. Makes them current. Within
the structure of present opinion & belief. Buildings
that now stand like skeletons (or holes in the ground) will
become meaty with walls & plumbing. In our excitement,
we may not consider that what is gone grows on without us.
We may not hear the hoary-haired individual say, "Oh sure,
I know where that is, you mean where the old pyramid building
used to be." Boom! We are carriers of each other's identity.
At each moment, we choose who we are & who agrees.

THE FOLDED LIE, THE TRUTH UNFOLDS

for Edwin Markham
& W. H. Auden

The theory of evolution curls in a red tide
over Auschwitz, over & over. Fish belly up,
slap against the shore, awaiting the wizard
to turn them into possum. A step up the ladder
& another chance to draw from Community Chest.

How no one dared believe it. Yet for others
so logical. So methodical. One might say,
"So business as usual." The seeds we planted
at Sand Creek, at Wounded Knee, Evanston
over & over. How salvation would come in

completion. Who calls these rocks inanimate?
This Earthy dirt from which springs begonias
in late summer? How the past takes form, grows with us;
changes, no longer physical; yet neither are we,
the living present, that small 'trapped' sum.

We must speak of it often. How the Earth spins
as it circles the sun. I have seen the dead
buried. They will not be forgotten. No. Never.
After each & every memorial & museum &
renovated relic crumbles into dust, the dead will

continue to flow through us, blood cell & tissue,
the deeds we have done. The company that comes for dinner
each night will again tell us the great expense
of dredging up dinosaurs, how necessary
they are for bumper-to-bumper angst & whiplash

fortunes. It's a fact. My life   *is* easier
than John the Baptist's. But there (& here) in exclusion
the complications begin.   I will never believe it.
No. That if the theory is true, at one time &
one place, all has come to this
                                        & moves on

TRANSLATIONS FROM DON WON TON
A WHITE CHINESE

2

The trees are gnarled to the roots
You stub your toe & hop on one foot, cursing.

Think of it this way: I say
knowing the self is enlightenment.

You chase me down the path

3

Armies cross your heart in moonlight.
Naked, they can barely stand

                            the discipline.
Strands of your hair command attention;
each gets what it wants,

                              shimmering, at ease
around the gravity of your face.
There is a call to arms.
         I pull you down to me.
Tips of your hair tickle my cheeks.
I tell you: the sage has said: *and those who conquer*
                   conquer because they yield.
You whisper in my ear:
                     I know karate.

4

Returning is the motion, I thrust.
Yielding is the way, O God!
        I am that long
             & you are all around me.
The ten thousand things are born of being.
I name.

                  Returning the motion,
     not lost in the gift,

I plot the way back.
I am not being facetious
but thrust to face you with my being.
I name this moment
                    for my return.

5

He who stays where he is endures
the dinner, without tasting.
Chow mein noodles are strewn on your sweater
                    above your breasts.
Your mouth is big, how can you miss it?

Knowing others is wisdom.
I stay in my seat & regard you.
You slob :I think
& I desire to kiss you.
Perhaps I, too, will land on your breasts.

Perserverence is a sign of will power.
Everyone in the restaurant is looking
you spill the wine.
Mastering the self needs strength.
I grit my teeth,
hold tightly to my chair,
vow to work out with weights.
I smile at you as if nothing has happened.
You smile back—
                    I am aroused.
Pieces of almond are caught between your teeth.
You drop a chopstick & bend down to pick it up.

Straightening up, your shoulder catches the table.
My lap is at once: wet, hot & sticky.

To die but not to perish is to be eternally present:
say the sages.
This is love :I say: You are what I always wanted.
I embrace you
& feel the weight of you
                    as you step on my toe.

6

The clarity of the sky prevents its falling.
You point to a formation of geese.
I honk for your laughter.

The low is the foundation for the high.
I tell you the way your calves become ankles drives me wild.
Could you love an amputee   :you ask.

The ten thousand things are whole & alive.
Why do you ask that? I say,
my stomach queazy.

A firmness of the earth prevents its splitting.
You tell me I coddle the cripples around me
with my own fear of weakness.

The strength of the spirit prevents its being used up.
I say: let's fuck in a bed of broken fortunes.
As long as it's your back on the cookies :you reply.

All these things are in virtue of wholeness.
You point to a buzzard feasting on carrion.
I honk & you laugh.

7

I watch you walk away
vivisection is unlike me, but
            I am reminded of the Dragon
            at New Year's
(I love a parade!)
                              big head to the right
ducking to the left
                        to the right
where your long hair ends. . .

a synapse that fires my inner being

cherry bombs explode all around me
I am deaf
my eyes are everything
                          & with you

you push & shove to be first on the bus
I marvel at the power in your calves
        your technique
the sureness of T'ai Chi:
                   pulling the tiger by the tail
you make it on

there are so many of us: I scream:
& you alone,   I want to call mine!

the bus leaves in an opium cloud
I drop my eyes to the concrete
        3 coins in the gutter!
providence! :I think
it's time I consulted my Richard Wilhelm

Lines in italics from *Tao Te Ching* by Lau Tsu
        translated by Gia-Fu Feng and Jane English

SPRING

Spring   & for all the craziness
& death, I find I'm still in love
with, among others, myself

O, adventurers would find
me boring as they venture up their mountain
I'm no where near their trail, still
spring courses through me
like a fifth cup of coffee
in an hour

I walk monoxide sidewalks,
searching for something in the windows to redeem
my idle habits—mere objects
have never held me for long, unless
they have meaning to engage my wit,
otherwise they're just someone else's elevators
                going up to a price tag
I'm not willing to pay.   The traffic
(& yours truly)
always has had a mind of its own that honks
when it thinks it's right

Do I ignore responsibility? We can think we do
Everything that is done to/by/for us...
Well, we can choose the moon. It enters
our lives on such a regular basis
we nearly take it for "granite?" Then, one night
much like any other, except it's this night
under this deepening blue sky
with all its bright twinkling thisses
The...
                moon
appears—
big & pale
crescent yellow,
just above the hill—
reflecting off electric skyscraper windows...
Everything I feel tells me:
Honk! what is distance
when Spring is coursing through

MARY

for Paula Gunn Allen

in the beginning, the word
allowed her a mystery

the wind entered
Gabriel blew his horn

the Goddess was still alive
a fugitive from fearful kings

but he was a fugitive too
born from this wedlock

II

he denied her when she called
she ever virgin & mother

"a prophet is not without honor
except in his own country,

and among his own kin,
and in his own house"

not to be pre-empted
he did not consort with her

III

who were these women
named Mary? (a coincidence

the one called whore:
the priestess, who followed him?

or the other, the mother
of James & Salome, of Joseph

she saw the moved stone
they saw the angel, a young man

IV

this was his story, imposed
on the geography of the times

they saw (a different world)
what they were looking for. messiahs

must have been all over, abundant
as poets in an energy crisis

women deities scorned, a world
full of egotistical & vengeful gods

V

his story is cradled in her silence
the nativity, the pieta

she is the before & after
he is always adored & in her arms

she, ever the seed, the fertile soil
& the grain ever ripe

with continuity. he, a hybrid
another crop planted to save the soil

VI

"no one puts new wine into old wine skins"
yes, he denied her—

as he was denied by Simon called Peter
one name weaves through the gospel

like a trinity of the moon
reflecting. the Father, the Son...

but suggests the Holy Spirit a cipher
awaiting resurrection in a name of woman

YOUR HANDS

you, moonchild
believing in the stars
send soft and silent satellites
out into the space
around your body
as messengers of love
curiosity
and defense

your hands
these satellites
adrift
as if on the ocean you possess
that possesses you,
do not express
feelings you wish to share

but are
as much as your hands are
you, these feelings
I must hold them
tightly

SONATA

what use is
a rain barrel
in the summertime?

in its stillness
open to the weather
waiting for the rain

shrinking
splintering
falling apart

filling its cracks
with air
subtly, unnoticed

the molecules
swirling faster
in the summertime

clashing together
exchanging atoms
inside the barrel

in its stillness
open to the weather
waiting for the rain

shrinking
splintering
falling apart

filling its cracks
with air
subtly, unnoticed

the molecules
swirling faster
in the summertime

clashing together
exchanging atoms
creating new molecules

destroying old ones
quickly, quietly
inside the barrel

in its stillness
open to the weather
waiting for the rain

shrinking
splintering
falling apart

filling its cracks
with air
subtly, unnoticed

the molecules
swirling faster
in the summertime

clashing together
exchanging atoms
creating new molecules

destroying old ones
quickly, quietly
efficiently discreet

soon there will be rain

THE OPENING

The opening. As if someone slit the surface
of an overripe Earth & the juice just rose up
through the rock to reveal itself. Eel River, Fortuna.

You are here with friends. One who knows
the area. One who carries a field guide
with colored pictures of birds.
                                   You sit on the bank,
on boulders extending from the tangle of branches
you squeezed through to get here. A long left
(toward town) & a longer right slighted by the sun's glare.
Over there, across the way the river recedes
from the row of trees leaving a layered beach
complete with skipping stones.
                                   In winter
when the water is high & a darker shade of green,
those trees are tested. You think of the January failures
that contribute to this June panorama...

Suddenly, a bird bursts from the bushes cutting
the air with uneven geometry, flurry & dash,
dart. "Definitely a swallow," your friend says
leafing quickly through the book. "Here, this one—
a barn swallow, the rust-colored breast..."
This amazes you, not for the naming but what is not:
trees, bushes, birds you can hear, boulders & rocks...
The vision extends into the shadows of the shapes
you feel. Coming from within. Something deeper
than the sense of it (or any pronoun.) Like calm.
An immediate knowing. That feeling, Angels.
The synchronicity extends through out...

Molecule. Subatomic particle. The long loping phrase
of a great blue heron heading west... To know each
& every name & to speak them in a moment. The moment:
unnamed, unknown. & still we try & often we extend
what we know. Always we go beyond this—
into the realm of Angels. The siren song the silence
presents to us.
                                   Circles in a river.
What a mouthful this swallow is. How it dips,

dives its beak into the water. The drops slip &
slam against the surface, reuniting the river in our eye
to our heartbeats & our souls... How we are carried
by this current to bend, to swell, to rush & to loose
these selves into that ocean that curls upon itself
to greet us. The Angels' song permeates all
from timeless within. Moving in & out of focus,
in & out of form. Like those drops my swallow spills.

★

I know nothing but this feeling. To have it broken
like that row of trees. A whole in the middle
where mountains miles away rise, stunning
in their great green coats. How it all changes...
The higher flying heron replaced by the kingfisher
looking for a meal. The river's the constant
& the river isn't, as sun sparkles from the bobbing
current crests. The process of choice.
I wonder what my eye sees in its own completeness.
This feeling remains, joyous in its own...

Like Jet Lag

Like jet lag. The pull from an unknown.
The connection, abstracted & otherwise
taken for granted, is within-geography.
The gravity of this situation is not grave

& gray matter, my blue skies, is the point
of departure. I am air born.
These hills I dwell upon are the wavelengths
of my soul. I do not strive for mountain tops

but find elevation in speaking from my heart.
My words are layered & ringed. Redwood trees
rooted to the Earth but from another source.
My body quakes like a wind-loosed branch

each time I say good-bye. An Angel falls.

POW-WOW

for Paula Gunn Allen
& Carol Lee Sanchez

Pow-wow. A convergence. I bring the Angels here.
They were here all the time, though I didn't know—
didn't recognize them as such—wanting something
everyone could see, like fry bread & beans.

People, nations & ways dancing to the drum.
A center. It is not mine, not here, not in this life.
I cannot dance. It would not be right. & so
I watch. Look in. Friends dance, claiming a who

they are. Each of us reaching in our own way, out
& in, to the center we create continually
from what we know of being & what we don't...
I created the Angels to center myself. Like Earth,

on one level. An event growing out of other events
not necessarily occurring in time. Or being
the effect of any visible cause. The silence
between drumbeats. The movement beyond the steps.

What I was becomes a symbol. & I am changing
flesh, moving away from child's sorrow, wanting
to lighten my heart with love, to trust the rainbow
I have created. Tearing open the spaces, I dance

in-conspicuously. Apart. & a part of the silence,
the movement, the dance that continues...

EURYDICE DISJOINT

She covers her place with rock radio. The wall
to wall sound changes the all-too-familiar
night into fused patterns of time. She can close
her eyes. The world with her lover disappears

behind a bottle of echoes & fog. She is deep
into the maze she lets her mind go, transported
by bottle, bass & drums. She kicks up her knees.
Frightened or defiant, she dances alone.

Wounds surround her space like air waves.
She tunes them in… I follow her into the slur
of past particulars. I'm not invited, rather converted
to a voice of the dead. Her sadness is

not known to me by word alone. We dance,
"the music" carries us into fragments of self-
strobed postures & memories… Taper, garlic, lace.
We neglect each reflection. If I am her lover,

I was. We did not see the light of day. To say
"She turned to choose the world she used to"
is incomplete. We mirror each other very well.
I'm looking back now & alas, we were both in hell

CEZANNE'S APPLES

il s'appelle Cezanne

a simple idea
scandalous for its time

man's abstractions
conscious upon the accepted
image of "nature"

Aphrodite coming
out of SF Bay
naked as Treasure Island
before the fair

nature morte avec pommes (still life with poems)
because isolation doesn't occur in nature
different planes of existence
create an archaeology that builds
a civilization of perspective

Cezanne's "tasteless"
apples naturally roll up
to computers
a bite taken
by megabyte motivation
upon a rumpled tablecloth

GRAND CANYON SHARDS

Jagged edges
layer into a cottonwood
of time.   Immediate knowledge.
My first look & all my words of iron
oxidize in my throat…

…A mile down, a little less—
I choose a rock to sit on, my feet dangling,
my head atilt, watching
a black crow fly; its wings pushing
your blue depth. The whoosh—
so loud— suspends me…
I'm falling… I'm not.
I look at the red rockface nearest me,
I want to live, to find again
my center.
Not yours, canyon, you're too self-assured.
That's an aspect of your grand allure…

The cool green morning air suggested
                only your agelessness.
It did not argue a later moment's dry wit:
Bright Angel, that step by step
descent into the fissure-
ridden rainbow.
Beauty erupts, spreading its fire
to gray squirrels & tarantulas. Wishing
to wash myself in your river,
I didn't fathom the yellow of your desert.
How quickly the fear of
Edward Munch's "Scream" approaches
                with thirst & buckwheat…

Your mirror: ages run through
my elements,
stratified by golden memories
carefully selected (if unconsciously)
& carried
to assume with confidence a who I am.
& there is so much
more, hidden by bluff
or purple promontory...

I stop short, (witness the work—
milleniums compressed here, this snow white
beauty seems so painful & slow)
yet only experience can etch
real these openings
              created through switchbacks
                        & parallax visions...

After, I ache with the knowledge
I've always been part of you;
I die here.
& my death is significant
as a pass from a pesty horse fly...

BLUE ANGEL

Blue Angel, I'm overwhelmed—
not by any Dietrich qualities
or Hollywood allure. . .
This is San Francisco, planet Earth.

Full moon, May 26, 1983.
The impersonal request. Circumstances
too complex to comprehend.
My heart beats. . . (a blue flame)

Call it instinct.
My need to piece together.
To shrink
the whole into beliefs. Straight lines

& corners. Soon, I'm phased out.
With worlds I'm not sure of
seeing.   This darkness
that holds remembrance of light.

New moon, blue moon—
a good time to plant, if the season's right. . .
If not—jilted,
a doddering professor with old answers

to sacrifice for a drink.
The rejuvenating cup
& a world dizzy with mystery
growing inside-out

& spilling back into myself. . .
The accelerated exhilaration, slow
as the ocean is slowly inevitable.
The next morning. . .

I'm not alone—
a pale & isolated orb in azure
where brave men go to look back
& sing praises of technology.

I too sing these praises
for I am full of praise for nearly everything
that casts light on
the indivisible web of reflection

CHOICES

Mysteries…
even choices
cannot be explained
away

       ★ ★ ★ ★ ★ ★ ★

One moment
follows
       the next, when
it isn't over
lapping
       interloping

I splinters
a Chinese sprinter onto

A new wheel
a gear not recog-
nized, in.   This Life

. . . a Whole
remembers
I feeds
      fills me
          insights & incidents
I don't believe in coincidence
My world's too subjective for That

       ★ ★ ★ ★ ★ ★ ★

FRIENDS

How beautiful to die
when death is not the end

She left me
& the beginning was water-torn
How tied I was— to
the things of we. Boxes
in the closet, weighted
& waiting to become part of
her again. The wanted

I wanted to be left alone—
unemcumbered by anything but the
roundness of the moment

The tree arrived as metaphor
Two friends on weekends
like bookends bracing
My three cents worth:
the I Ching said Retreat

★

Once having circled there
what can be said of the dark
side of the moon

★

Given: the tree could grow
straight, at any angle
or die; even as is,
could avoid the attention
& didn't— in our world
There are so many trees to choose

So much here
lifts as if to face
the sun

These moments are golden
So many songs. & wanting to
understand, we rely on limits, create
an ideal to hold on to, an image
to hold up (to) the world
This is not knowing, this is
creating. This is not control,
but a longing to part-take

Always a part of us
feeling the stretch, somewhere
the singer, somewhere the song

★

When the tears are over
& we have found the personal
as profound as the classic
tragedy, do we weep some more
for our good fortune

★

So many songs. A cacophony
& wanting to… We can
forget ourselves in our interest
She loves me not. She loves…
& you? At this moment forgetting
the chorus can be deafening
even in the quietest refrains

No fight, no flight. I am of them
as I am myself: indivi-duality
An in-tension I can project out:
my desire to love & yet,
this is the season to let go
Because she is free, I am
only pointing out the alignment
Love is not linear, it lifts
by reflection, even in the shade of a tree
Symbolic or no. Friends pre-sent
a minder & re-, I'm not in the past

Awake, the dream
continues on. Both real-
I-ties remain true for me. I
choose one. Here.

PERSEPHONE

Persephone arises
from the underworld in her
search for completeness

Why then this sorrow,
this weakness?
Am I not Hades?
Is not this darkness of my own making?

Yes, & again, there is a sense
strong as pain
of not having known her—
that she, the bringer of light so bright,
could disappear so quickly,
just change her mind
& darkness   Damn, Angel—
she was such sweetness
Who is this woman that walks away?
Who did I know?
She was always free to go…

★   ★   ★   ★   ★

It is said I abducted her

It is true   I encouraged
her   move away from Mother
The seed was planted
The choice was hers   Is hers—

She says only "it is time"
There is no warning
& there was—
but it was visible
only to hindsight, hiding in symbols
needing an event to make them

clear   She leaves
Who can dispute it? I call her
Queen of the Underworld

★   ★   ★   ★   ★

The choice was hers—
we made it together

She moves toward
Demeter, the surface,
the moonlit landscape that compels her
I have given myself & whatever that is
for her, she takes with her—
not simply as memory, I have touched
the subtler places as well   I know
for she has touched them in me
& given them light

She ran out of my image of her,
the beautiful The comfortably known
Now, this darkness…
Forgotten, the net
of knotted times, the probable
paths we take to make Self
bigger than a life

"Lord of Darkness"
It becomes me at times

★   ★   ★   ★   ★

She is like many of us:

as wonderfully expressive as she is
she cannot say it all…

She holds things inside
that do not fit
the mood she deems appropriate
& then, only her emotions are true;
the rest is a blur…

She moves out of relation
with the world that crumbles—

she can say, "Look, this isn't real,
this isn't necessary,
                        it breaks so easily,…"

& her logic is impeccable
She forgets herself

until it is time to remember again
then she is sad

then she is bright & beautiful
then she can seem mortal again

$$\star \quad \star \quad \star \quad \star \quad \star$$

Persephone—
She is/the fruit of the underworld,
a mystery that deepens, beckons
holds us speechless

                        if for an instant only

            to break

It is her nature not to be swayed
but to venture a present so powerful
it has no past

She inspires—
little understanding, rather leaves us
to accept
                        we have made a choice
Something Orpheus tolerated
only when darkness concealed his movement
(Beauty may be misleading here)
Given the light, it was maddening—
a true love did not stop him from turning
the one sown seed into a great song
of sorrow

It was Persephone's visage
he carried when he left us
Having entered full of prowess,

he did not reckon her majesty
He didn't believe   He couldn't   He wanted
to know what would happen next...
the moment to last forever...
& so blind, he did as she said   He waited,
concentrated, hoping to gain some insight,
some sense of her that would make her real,
relatable   His beloved Eurydice, paled,
a ghost not even considered

When the sun caught his eye, he awoke—
a world he could judge, he wanted to,
had to see her in the light
he knew. Only Persephone in his mind,
he turned   He could see
was she really the way he remembered...

The turning   Thoughts
of Eurydice fading...   & the remembering
He forgot what he couldn't believe
He knew only sorrow & shame
—then came his song

That spell she weaves...
When I faced her beauty, ...yes, I wanted
When I faced her woman, ...O, I needed
& without knowing how, my power was less
No, I wasn't powerless; I still created *my* world,
but now she was always considered   A part of me
grew, a part died   Some say: Shame
Old Hades, the abductor of an innocent child
gathering flowers with girl friends
Daughter of Demeter, goddess of all
that lives & grows, darkness becomes her:
She plucks the blooms of this world

If I rule here, it is by distancing & reflection;
I am seed & time   Demeter is the fertile source:
mother & daughter are one   It became obvious—
we had not stepped off the chariot
when the gardens rang with her moaning:
"Persephone in the underworld & grief
upon the Earth"   Ancient Gaia is forgotten

The seeds to many actions are sown in the fields
below Olympus…   I've had a million great &
foolish adventures no mortal's taken the time
to re-call, …distort   I could've been
a husband desparately sought & found
What I did, I chose to do
& the mortals chose to remember
They had their reasons   & desires
Some say in taking Persephone for my wife
I conquered a Mother-right culture
They listen too much to Zeus' boasts,
judging the rest of us minor thunder-bearers
They forget immortal nature
Persephone was always free, she chose to be
the source of my desire & undivided in her loves
& thus, able to make connections
mortal Orpheus could not,
coming from the possessive realm of
Demeter's abundant creativity

I am & always was called husband
Adonis is always her lover

Greek to Me

Half of me is third generation.

"I shall tell you more. There is no birth in mortal things & no
end in ruinous death. There is only mingling & interchange of
parts, & it is this that we call 'nature.'" (Empedocles)

This country is founded on Protestant principles.
He kept singing "We Shall Overcome"
as he marched through concrete streets &
heard his words echo off the walls
of government & the dead
bodies that lie within the lines
the electron gun fired upon the picture tube
into his brain
                        until he was hoarse & crying.
Little mingling occurred.
He was at war with a world at war
& no less explosive.
Thinking back, it was the catholicity of the experience
I abhor.

Though half of me is third generation,
all of me was born here & continues to be.

"Into the same river, I step & do not step." (Heraclitus)

Authorities were immediately defensive
"There is no danger." Instruments read, reflected:
something beyond the senses is happening here
that cannot be explained
mathematically. The pope is Polish.
In the home for unwanted ideas, a leader,
whose time has come, gets up on an orange crate
& beckons others:
                        "Reclaim yourself."
At once, gangs of ideas roam the night streets looking
for love & a place to hang out. Emotion literally squeals to
                        [be seen, as it races up & down narrow avenues

46

boxed in metal. Almost nostalgically,
the unwanted become feared;
their exuberance incomprehensible to a solid-state system.
Not even the suggestion of an Excedrin headache seems
                              [to calm these urges into respectability.
A tornado in Texas, an earthquake in San Francisco,
these are to be expected at times like this.
Foundations are moving!

"I am the most widely travelled man of all my contemporaries,
& have pursued inquiries in the most distant places; I have
visited more countries and climes than anyone else, & have
listened to the teachings of more learned men. No one has
surpassed me in the drawing of lines accompanied by
demonstrations, not even the rope-knotters of Egypt, with whom
I passed five years on foreign soil…I came to Athens & no one
knew me."   (Democritus)

HOMAGE TO GOYA

1

a declaration

accompanies each (caprice)
how it manifests—

no Sistine Chapel
of accomplishment
yet each is perfect

I picture Goya (in top hat)
laughing as he penned
his dis- (or re-)coveries
—an eternity

this reality
is reality—(clear
as Who are you Now
Time's an element
grotesquely savored

2

the jargon is awk
ward at first & "more,
better, different"
enticing with its
promises of trans

formation   You learn
it can be another
new place to hide if
there isn't action
(& note: not re- like

traditional culture)
there's plenty: this is
natural, how it
is, always will be
There's no Eureka

but to move ahead
Unblind your vision
"The dream of reason
produces monsters"
& no indivi

duality Ac(t)-
knowledge these dark creatures
(who) survive in comfort
zones with or without
cause, special effects

3

Indivisible
duality*, I
or we, the golden
rule is a rule &
decodes the mirror

I face I can see
Goya crying, etched
in aquatint & blue
honesty a rule's
not something to be

followed but measures
"this is" These monsters
grow in my resignation,
ignorance or "low
self-esteem" Be true

* — "indivisible duality," a phrase coined by Paula Gunn Allen by splitting "individuality" into "indivi-duality" during a conversation I had with the poet/writer. I heard it as a spiritual/unconscious etymology.

"All (the flying ones)
will fall," decoyed down
by Earthy passion
they claim to eschew
til they are nabbed &

shaken, shame's "plucking"
awakes the Adam
who must leave Eden's
"self" for a cosmos
of green ironies

4

I want so to write
anthems that inspire
yet Frankenstein trods (often)
where Baryshnikov
could leap to glory

please stand by, this
experiencing is
difficult Each moment
has its tints & shades
"You cannot escape"

survival context
the young girl dances
before winged ghouls
no fear in her face
yet she knows they're there

Goya's painter is
a monkey, his model's
an ass, he counsels
"Neither more nor less"
His center's the brush

the dancer stretches
absorbed within art,
an ambiguous
language, yet she has
surrendered to it

5

fear or excitement
same experience
different label
yes, I can re-treat
to Goya's ago

but this poem says
also, all time is
simultaneous
a man with no teeth
looks sad, desirous

at a young woman
his hands are tied for
he assists a crone
with her wool-spinning
the woman, coy, leans

back, her hands gathered
in front of her sex
a translation reads
"It's better to do
nothing" my ego

reacts—he's got to
cut the wool…Goya,
your wise old crone is
laughing It's tragic
desire satisfied!

BILLBOARD

*Once this was all
black plasma
and imagination*
—Michael McClure

*Because things are how we relate to this existence,
that's why!*

words are a poem
even on a billboard
above Union Square

brings a romance
a call
touches me
some inner place
& my body is a wash of chemicals
dormant a moment before

I saw a pigeon descend
across the December sun
& a voice came from a radio
& it could have said almost anything,
I wasn't listening,
for the waters that swept over me…

I AM
well pleased to be alive,
& a part of this rite
this multitude

ASSOCIATIONS

"I'm breaking down, Man…
Really… I'm breaking down."
A boy. Homeless
Dirty. Tears in his eyes
Just pushed away
from a garbage can
by a shopkeeper's broom
The shopkeeper isn't wrong
He's fighting for his gold mountain, too
& he can't bear to see
a part of his self
down so low
It's one of those associations
you don't like to make in your head
Like me,
I just listen to
"All I wanted is some bread, Man"
& I drop a few coins in his palm
I'm not right
Nothing's changed
The pain, I feel it
& I throw money at it
Not wanting to stay there. Not knowing
what else I can do…
& live my own dreams
I feel blessed &
there is no void
I turn the corner
"Change, Bro?"

THE GODDESS OF WALNUTS

My grandfather planted these
three walnut trees many years before
I was born. In some mythology
there is a goddess of walnuts.
Call her Shelley. I've seen a picture—
my grandfather, a shovel
in his hands. Pride, passion:
a young man posing, standing next to
a sprig of a tree. My father
must've been three/four years old.
This moment tolls, rings of generation.
A form of meditation. Gathering
nuts, quietly engrossed on the Other.

Shelley would have to be a goddess.
She is a miracle of air, rain, soil & sun
particularized within/her chamber shelters
her creations from these very forces that shape
& nourish. Only last year my father
in that army coat he wore
when he worked out in the yard, so nimble
on one limb, shaking another or both.
I'm so unsure today. Bending down
to collect the nuts, the lower back stretches
the legs. How arbitrary these distinctions,
we make them so important. More important
than an immensity we fear is chaos, is
the end of us. Nuts dropping from the heavens, space
undefined six months ago. Without the seasons,
how would the branches employ the wind?

I'm not speaking history, third person
singular, but mystery, the first.
I use to fear pain. I don't
embrace it now. At the moment I write
I feel it is a part of me, a sweet sadness
I cannot explain reverberates through my past

as if I always knew. The way the wind
whips the branches/spring back. Thinking
of deities, so much is left in abstraction.
She is the nut meat, its shape, the shell; she is
also the pain I feel—a leaf cut off from
the roots, memory that has no home.
That nourishment. & though it appears
a plaything of the wind, memory is a force
that shelters & grounds. Feeling is set off;
she tastes so real, though in no way is she human.
To understand her thus is to destroy
something we do not understand…

The same rain that weighs the leaves
to fall, feeds the spring/growth…
She is the seasons as Earth is the moon.
For sixteen days in summer, I was caught up in
his momentum. His unrelenting hyperventilations
of thought & breath. My father becoming crone
taught me: understanding must sometimes bow
to acceptance. There was nothing else we could do
in that probability. Those who come back,
speak of rising above the shape, a light
& the choice. More than language connects
the nuts of the walnut tree/from one year
to any other. I felt so alone, though not separated
from his final choice. Shelley is an intelligence
that combines & then holds together.
A purpose   …if I enjoy one nut   …if I don't.
Winter approaches: the tree is nearly leafless
& will certainly go on producing. I confess:
I came back, I chose to live
in a world with walnuts. & if they are not my favorite,
I do enjoy the taste these memories bring
a time before Shelley created herself
though she always was & he always will be

The Dark Maid

she is the dark maid who lives in the tree
we do not want her, we do not want her, they say
she does not love us, she does not wish us well

let there be light, ...& there was light
but she was blind & bed-ridden
screaming inanities
for they did not respond to her pain

she is the dark maid in the trunk of the tree
she is the older sister, the first wife we fail
to mention, the wife who turns to salt
(the second wife was civil enough, we could blame her)

and the light was good
and so many threw the first stone
it became an industry

she is the dark maid in the hallupu tree,
the exile, the expelled who rules the barren land
the one who braves the ocean to flee the tyrant
the one who finds no safe harbor

she was old & troublesome
living between two worlds, unwilling
to find a simple solution

THE PROBLEM

I

She falls—
the wailing wall of grief

She descends
& rends the old world into memory
but has no will to create her world anew

He has left
her hobbling & blind to the mystery
beating her chest in a watery void
with no god to speak of or to

II

I slip back—
a time I thought her the creator

Alone with this Inanna in descent…
my life is interrupted
mid-discourse on goddesses in my life

How obvious—the way she assumes
authority, the badge
she carries: "Mother-in-distress"
No mistaking our signature

III

War rages in Lebanon…
The city in tatters

How long has it lasted now—
offering a perspective for matters not
so bloody, as this intent

She is in her hour of need &
I cannot help her   So many "colored suns"
have exploded on the landscape
Noise distracts us from our bonding

IV

Once of one flesh/she became a voice
to lash out against for betrayal

a disjunction of dreams/a force to tear
away from/this perspective is passing
& it can only be a miracle

"I didn't ask to be born"
curses cousin derelict lost in his seclusion
amid the passers by   …I turn away
That is exactly what I'm not trying to say

V

She has lost him & nothing I do
can bring him back   "Bring him back"

she screams, not at me, but the god
she rejects—she can't imagine
her pain/part of anyone's plan/she'd worship:

she says "I'm numb"   …& it's true
anything I could say she would counter:
"You don't understand"   Ah, yes…
but is that really what's important?

VI

They have preached: believe in Him
Okay, I believe in Her also as transcendent,

a force beyond the circumstance of the fertile
bulging belly   In this life, I came through her,
called Mother   Yes, it was my desire & she fulfilled

those wishes   I am grateful & continue to be
the primary creative force in my own life
The question becomes: Who now is this
"I,"   anyone's "I"?

VII

To hear the President talk
there can be no middle ground

in Central America   It's our right to impose
"the way" because we gave money
to someone & ourselves/permission on paper

some time ago & no, I will not be sacrificed
for a duplicitous society   Murder never led to
True freedom cannot be protected but created
one by one in a concerted commitment as goal

VIII

You were there for me always trying
to fill my needs as if they were simple,

a matter of thirst, & now you are in need
& I simply do not have that same desire
preferring to nurture a relationship of two

independent individuals   I've inherited a lot
from you, I'm learning more about that
each day   Looking back, your love made it
safe, not easy, to rebel against your values

IX

A friend's wisdom consoles
as it voices perspectives:

When I can't stand my own
kids, ... they're most like me
Something they've taken here

they've warped [getting it] there
It's recognizable... & wrong
All consuming, clarity of intent
is at stake (burning)/& the world is new

X

Time heals   These moments—a pot on the stove,
intensely anticipated vapors, something

that registers a change   We give a lot
& I'm amazed at your deftness, a world
emerges from pain, memory   Slowly,

slowly, slowly life rebuilds itself,
in fact, grows over untended intentions   Two people
feeling a desire to mesh but finding themselves
alone   Love is not the problem

AN AMERICAN LEARNS THE GREEK GODS

The gods
move easy
in this place
riding the sounds
of traffic

Zeus
hangs ten
on the waves
of a hook
& ladder
siren

Brother Hades
prefers
an ambulance
scream
in crisis
as does Persephone
when she isn't rumbling
& screeching
with her mother
above a muni-bus

Ares rides
police cars
but wishes
they drove
loud monster
trucks
with big tires

Or course,
Hermes
steals
every
Harley
on the street

Aphrodite
prefers
the pleasurable purr
of a limo
off the stoplight

while Artemis
takes pleasure
in the whining
engines
of sports cars
with four on the floor
athletically
maneuvering
in & out
of traffic

Dionysus
will take any car
that's DUI
or driving recklessly
or even a car
that backfires
now
& again

Athene
sits atop
a quiet
efficient
Mercedes
while Hera
takes taxis
through
the red light
districts
& abuses
the horn

Apollo
judges his cars
by their radios
(volume up
loud!)
changing stations
often to create
coded messages
with the
pushbuttons .

In the distance
not so far
from this street scene
Poseideon offers
his eternal presence
through
a foghorn.

AT MY MOTHER'S BEDSIDE

At your bedside, it helps
to see flames lap up the log of your life

That hearth is warm in this winter season
I still cannot stay too long or get too close

the intense heat—
a fundamental lesson of childhood

I must kiss you, knowing

You do not see blue tongues consume your flesh
You taste nothing at this feast
Your saliva has dried up & your thoughts explode
    like once-thick sap

You do not hear the quick crackle
& pop as you speak
from the insatiable place
saying you only want water
& the pain to cease

you only want water & the pain to cease
you only want water & the pain to cease

Do you smell the smoke of time rise
to a senseless epiphany?

At this moment my simple vision sooths me
can it help you, do I need to?
You are the fire
I am

NOTRE DAME

I must begin this
just outside *Notre Dame*,
maybe forty feet
like forty days & forty nights

The dream I had last night
drawn back repeatedly
I could not present this poem
Others there were ready
I was not
Each time I stood
in front, I disappeared
& there was Wil to retrieve me
& once again
I could not present this poem

this could mean many things
as now, the doors are closed

———————

(2 days later, inside the cathedral)

I think I was afraid to speak it
to make some sense
of this warm sorrow
that holds me to her
All would be lost
in some pithy simplicity
that outlined the light
& ignored the dark altogether

Mother & child have importance here
Inside, between the roses
she wears a crown
in lieu of a halo
The babe is in her left hand
She carries a scepter—
a lily or a candle?—in her right
(All express light)

The babe carries the orb
His right arm looks clumsy on his mother's collarbone/tunic
No emotion on either of their faces
just a long look through the ages
—a reason for hope
This is my mother's church
She would have loved it here, far from Petaluma
a sanctuary of stone & glass, wood & wicker
Mankind striving for beauty & solace

She could never give up or let go
                    being "mother"
Maybe I can understand that a little more today

I light a candle to her memory in her church
& walk out alone

----

background:
Mom's mother died in childbirth
two weeks after she was born
when Mom was pregnant,
the dr. told her she might have the same problem
she chose to go ahead with the birth

from a notebook, dated 5-30-94:

a whale swam up the Petaluma River

I was born in 1949, it is now 1994
numerically, Mom did what she feared doing:
she died two weeks after my birthday
these 45 years were her blessing!

the last thing she said to me
she asked for my forgiveness

she died 3 years to the day
she arrived at the rest home

the whale disappeared the day Mom died

———————

(that night – as a service is going on in Sacre Coere)

It doesn't seem complete
There was another aspect, the other altar
the *pieta*

She holds her arms out to the world
                    in her grief
This is an aspect of the Mother too

the great Mother
the mother that the patriarchy couldn't kill
So they gave her son the last judgement
but yes, here it is he
who lies dead in her arms
                    the arms of this earth
                    the arms of this world

She who symbolized consciousness of this world
opens out, in her grief,
to symbolize consciousness in the Other

& yet, this is not my case
I cannot hold my arms out
as she does
            I am child
            who has survived
I grieve—yes
but I cannot give solace to the world
I can only remember the love she gave me
the mystery of it
the selflessness (at times)
(that struggle with a wounded self—
her mother lost to her
                        (her father unavailable)
No matter how many times I lashed out against her
            in my frustration & unknowing
that selflessness returned

& on the last day I saw her alive
we cried in each other's arms & said I love you

as if we knew
but after 3 years,
like 3 days & 3 nights, I didn't
—consciously

July 1–3, 1995

SONG OF ALMAGEST

for Doreen Stock

dead center
in the living universe, I am
      Ptolemy finally going around the sun

a bird sings
my feet on the ground, the Earth
      there had been silence
      it was necessary
            gravitational involvement perhaps
a beautiful clear voice
      relative to none – silence shattering

★★★

a beautiful clear night
      relative to none – the Milky Way
& other galaxies pulsate their light (Andromeda is our neighbor)
         explosions of energy
– inter-galactic collisions (emissions -
             fusions) a star is creating itself
      – the universal factory
      the cosmic heap
         LOST! in vacuous void
           of twinkling
blackness

the mammalian eye, the human ear
      blind and deaf
         dumb-founded for expressions
      neck muscles tilted back, looking up
         aware of the skin of existence
         aware of the I

through nebulous clarity
                              bright stars shine, evolve
each with the power to light a million moons
each with the power to bring starless day
                to the planets it lords over

                              ★★★

                                        listen,
                        here/now explains my error—
        the bird's sweet song is heard over the sun's thunder...

Bill Vartnaw, circa 1989

Praise for *Suburbs of My Childhood*

"Bill Vartnaw has written a splendid book. It starts quietly, with observations on several small beasts, kittycats whose silent absolutely impenetrable actions are noted; then, with scant (but sufficient) notice, the author finds himself called upon to trace the troubles between Hades and Persephone, whose tragedy is to live only in the present. Bill sees this very clearly and I found his writing to be clearer even than Robert Duncan's, the last I read for this classic information. Then the poem grows personal to end with, detailing the death of a matriarch of Bill's clan and her funeral processes. This is all done in up-to-date language, so that the poems both epic and modern are capable of being read. It is a thrilling story of heroes bewildered by the gods and the best writing of its kind to come my way for many a year."
 —David Bromige
  author of *as in T as in Tether*

  "I come to this life to leave my fingerprints ..." ("The Pursuit")

"As Editor & Publisher of Taurean Horn Press, Bill Vartnaw has presented the works of other poets to the community at large for many years. He has also presented his own written works to the community both orally & in published form. Readers of this collection of Bill's Poetry will discover his particularly interesting way of sharing aspects of his life & views—thru Poetry—with his readers. He tells us in "Contact Sport" ... "at each moment we choose who we are and who agrees..." I for one agree with his choice of Poet having heard him read in public many times & I'm sure readers of this collection of Bill's Poetry will enjoy it as I have."
 —Carol Lee Sanchez-Allen
  author of *Rainbow Visions* and *Earth Ways*

"As for yr manuscript, don't wanna be redundant but it's direct & tender & alert to difficulty w/out making the words get in the way. I received it w/ recognition of its modest subtlety & yr eye for delight & light. Thank you."
 —David Meltzer
  author of *David's Copy, The Selected Poems of David Meltzer*